Ham's Christmas Communion

To Bryan, a wonderful nephew and devoted Christian servant!
Bill Bryan

B. L. BRYAN (Uncle Bill)

ILLUSTRATED BY PAUL BRYAN

Merry Christmas Bryan.
Paul 2004

Advantage INSPIRATIONAL™

Ham's Christmas Communion by B. L. Bryan

Copyright © 2004 by Bill L. Bryan
All Rights Reserved
ISBN: 09754332-4-5

Published by: ADVANTAGE BOOKS
            www.advbooks.com

Library of Congress Control Number: 2004113568

First Printing: November 2004
Cover and Interior Illustrations by Paul Bryan

04 05 06 07 08 09 10   8 7 6 5 4 3 2 1

Printed in the United States of America

Acknowledgements

This story was a long time in developing. It was begun in 1995 and laid aside with the intent to finish it soon. That did not happe, however, until eight years later. On taking it up again I discovered that the main idea was still alive and begging for completion.

I wish to acknowledge the encourage-ment I have received from my wife, Erma, and also the interest and support from my colleagues on the staff at Grace United Methodist Church in Naperville.

Special thanks are due to my son, Paul who shared his talent and a great deal of his time in drawing the sketches.

Also, I am very greatful to Michael Janiczek and his staff at Advantage Books for all their assistance and their prompt response to my many questions.

4

Foreword

Ham's Christmas Communion is the story of a farmer who has become embittered, selfish, and isolated from his community following the death of his wife many years earlier.

Just before Christmas a strange dog comes to his doorstep. Ham is angered by this and takes the dog several miles away and releases him. But on Christmas eve, the dog comes back again and gets entangled in the fence by the farm pond.

In releasing the dog from the fence and taping up his wounded legs, a renewed impulse for community enters Ham's spirit, prompting him to go to the late night communion service at the church where his cold heart is melted.

Ham's Christmas Communion

HAMILTON CARREL'S HOUSE STOOD WELL KEPT BUT STARK IN ITS TREELESS YARD ON SAND CREEK ROAD. Its lack of hominess and the general severity of the place matched him well, for he liked to use his hands to shape things straight and true since his relational world was devoid of warmth. People called him Ham, and that was perhaps fitting

8

for there were indeed several pig-like quali-
ties about him. None of the other farmers
would trade work with him, and when he was
desperate for extra help—say to get his alfal-
fa into the barn before predicted rains or to
get his corn in the crib before the coldest
days of the winter—he would hire one of the
Eldmar boys who liked to live wild and were
always looking for more money. The Eldmars
were willing to risk being cheated, and if you
didn't want to be cheated it was said you
stayed away from Ham. This reputation was
not entirely fair, or was surely worse than the
actual facts. But like bad reputations do, it
lived. Bob Sarvers who fancied himself clever
used to say that Ham almost sold his soul to
the devil once, but the devil backed out, not
wanting to get the worst end of the deal. And
then Sarvers would throw back his head and
laugh as though he were the greatest wit in
the county. Others lacked appreciation for
his humor.

Ham Carrel had not always been the way

9

10

he was. Thirty years earlier, before Josie died, Ham was as outgoing and sharing as any man around. The older folks in Sand Creek township remembered well how he used to be.

"What a shame," they would say shaking their heads, "That he turned so when his wife died."

But when Josie Carrel died, something broke inside Ham's spirit, and it appeared that it would never be mended. Sorrow had given way to self-pity, self-pity to anger, anger to bitterness, and bitterness to selfishness. On occasion, any or all these previous stages of his inner descent would reappear and walk like ghosts to haunt every possible relationship.

Except for the necessary selling of his produce and paying of his bills, he had gradually withdrawn from the community. No one cared very much. After intermittent attempts to break through the bitter wall and

11

reopen his closed heart had been rebuffed, the neighbors were content to let him be. It is sad to say it, but even the church had passed him by. When he had shaken hands with the preacher beside Josie's grave thirty years before, it was like a final Good Bye! to religion, and Ham had not set foot inside the church since. He was as near friendless as anyone could be.

One night only two days before Christmas at about 9:00 o'clock in the evening, Ham was seated in his big chair reading the paper. The fire in the fireplace had died down to some separated, glowing logs and an ascending ribbon or two of blue smoke. Finishing the reading, he dropped the paper to the floor and stared into the hot, orange rubble before him. His usual winter evening mood, a mixture of sulking loneliness and general dislike for the world, settled in. The disgust he felt at the trivia of the stories in the paper gradually gave way to drowsiness. Just as he was about to get up

13

from his chair to go to bed, he heard a sound, a sort of low moan coming from the opposite side of the room behind him. Then there was a second one, a louder one, accompanied by a bump on the door. He was startled at this. It had been a long time since anyone had knocked on his door—especially at 9:00 o'clock at night. Turning he noticed that the inner door leading into the small entry way was slightly ajar. Little wonder that the room had felt drafty or that he had heard the knock, if that was what it was, so clearly. He stepped into the entryway where coats and jackets of assorted weights hung on hooks and extra boots were setting on the floor in the corner. He opened the outside door a crack and peered through. There, laying on the stoop and huddled against the door, apparently to soak up what little warmth seeped through, was a large dog.

Ham was not a little disturbed at this beastly intrusion into the enjoyment of his misery. If there was anything he liked less than people, it was probably dogs.

"Git!" he yelled, opening the door further and stomping his foot on the threshold. At this the dog leapt up and moved quickly across the stoop and down the two steps to the snow covered walk. But there, surprisingly, he went no further, but rather turned and looked at Ham as though objecting to this breach of common civility. This exasperated Ham, and he grabbed the snow shovel from beside the door, banged it on the stoop, and with a louder yell ran down the steps at the dog, exposing himself to a blast of the frigid wind that was whipping around the southwest corner of the house. The dog, seemingly content to put only a few feet of space between himself and his aggressor, retreated a few more feet toward the front gate and again turned and stared at Ham. Ham was gathering strength for a second charge when he realized he was getting chilled to the bone through his flannel shirt and thin sweater vest. Seeing the ridiculous-

15

ness of his situation, with one final shout and a dramatic brandishment of the snow shovel, he turned and ran back into the house.

Where had this dog come from? It was too dark in the yard with only the light from the windows to get a good view of him. He didn't recall ever seeing him around the neighborhood or chasing cars in front of any of the farmhouses. Had someone from town dumped him out along the roadway? The idea angered Ham. Well, it didn't matter. A moment's thought assured him that all things at the back of the house, around the sheds, and at the barn were secure. There was nothing much he could hurt.

So Ham locked both the doors, went through the kitchen and checked the back door, pulled the fireplace screen tightly together, and made ready to climb the stairs. Before shutting off the light, he noticed the newspaper he had thrown aside laying in an untidy heap beside his big chair. He picked it

16

up and stacked it carefully with his magazines. Neatness of objects seemed very important to Ham, his relational world being pretty much askew. Newspapers and magazines could be stacked neatly and always stayed where they were placed. He liked them for that.

Just as he turned to go to the stairs, he heard the unwelcome guest in the yard sounding off in something that could be described as a cross between a yelp and a bark. It was a loud, intrusive yelp, as most yelps are, and Ham reflected a moment on the injustices of the human situation. He weighed his options. The inconsiderate beast would keep him awake all night. He thought of his old twelve-gauge leaning dutifully in the corner in the back entry way. It was an attractive alternative. But then, he thought the better of it. It was noisy and messy, would require going out into the cold to get the carcass out of sight before daylight, and possibly leave a big patch of frozen blood

19

which would likely stay in his front yard until the first warm day. No, the situation clearly called for something else. Then it came to him. He would clear out the front entry way and try to get the dog inside for the night. Perhaps once out of the bitter wind, the dog would be quiet. This would buy some time. He would decide on a long term solution in the morning.

He removed the coats and sweaters from the wall pegs in the entry way and set the boots and other items inside the living room. Then he opened the front door. The dog was standing on the stoop, and as soon as Ham backed away from the open door, he cautiously walked into the entry way—as anticipated. Man and animal stood and looked at each other with mutual disrespect. Now, with more light, Ham verified his earlier impression. He had never seen this dog before. He was a sort of dirty, reddish brown, clearly not an Irish setter. Obviously, a mixed breed. And he was without a collar and tags. He was about the ugliest creature Ham had ever seen, and for a fleeting moment he pictured himself going up and down Sand Creek road the next day trying to find a home for the miserable beast. The thought of such humiliation was about more than he could bear. Quickly then, he closed the front door and reentered the living room.

Another idea came to him. The dog was less likely to put up further fuss if he had something to eat and some water. Trying to assure himself that such action would be entirely practical and in no way compassionate, Ham went to the back entry way. He filled a small bucket with water from the laundry tub faucet, took it to the front, and set it before the dog, demonstrating that a charitable act is not always as charitable as it appears. He then remembered two potato cakes and a small piece of ham that he had left over from the day before. These also were placed in the hallway. The dog surveyed his new situation with interest, but his suspi

21

22

cions of Ham kept him from approaching the food. Ham closed the inner door and ascended the stairs to his room. His last thoughts were about what should be done the following day.

Upon arising at about 5:15, Ham poured out yesterday's coffee, wondering why he had left it in the pot, made some fresh, sliced some pieces of bacon, and cooked some cereal. He had not thought of the intrusive animal visitor from the night before until a whimpering sound from near the front door aroused his late sleeping memory. This morning, first thing, he promised himself he would get rid of the beast.

23

Finishing breakfast and hurrying out to feed the livestock, Ham turned the problem over in his mind. Finally he hit upon a plan. He had to drive over to Caldwell during the morning to the feed store to buy some supplement for the calves. This was perfect he thought. He would get the dog into the cab of the truck in some way, drive him five or six miles down the road and push him out by the abandoned Williams place where it was pretty much wooded on both sides of the road. There no one would see what he was doing. It should work fine.

When the feeding and other smaller chores were done, Ham worked his plan. He found some old rope and made a loop in the end to serve as a collar. He went into the house and through to the front entry way, closing the door behind him. The dog faced him in the confined space. In this plight the dog raised no protest as the loop was slipped over his head and tightened. It was a simple matter to lead him through the house and out the back. In alternate pushings and pullings he was able to get him up into the cab of the pickup. At the old Williams place Ham stopped the truck, glanced up and down the road, removed the noose, and pushed him out of the truck. He congratulated himself as he drove away toward Caldwell leaving

the dog standing in the roadway looking after him.

The remainder of the day passed quickly. After returning from Caldwell, he busied himself with moving some of the baled hay from one of the sheds to the barn and repairing some board fence and a gate at the feed lot. The small amount of snow on the ground did not hinder this, though the cold breeze which had come up caused some discomfort. The thought that it was Christmas eve crossed his mind a few times, to which he responded inwardly with his own version of "bah, humbug". Christmas held no interest for him. The loneliness of his life had long since been faced and conquered—or so he thought.

Following his supper, Ham sat before the fire and read the paper. He noted that there was a late communion service at the church. Ah yes, he thought to himself. It's Christmas. The hypocrites will gather. Then he started a

27

book. The heavy work in the cold of the afternoon and the warmth of the fire soon made him drowsy. He fell asleep. Though he stirred once or twice for a moment, he slept in the chair until well after ten o'clock. Once fully awake he tried to remember if he had locked the truck and closed the big door to the hay shed in case a blowing snow came during the night. Bundling himself against the cold and taking his five cell flashlight he went out the back. The breeze had died down a bit but the temperature had fallen sharply.

He was on his way back to the house when a yapping, howling sound was carried to him on the breeze from somewhere down beyond the feed lot. It was a disturbing, eerie sound. An animal was in pain he thought, probably caught in one of the fences. Then he remembered: the dog!

But that was impossible. He had left the dog more than five miles away by the old

Williams place. Yet in spite of its unlikeli-
hood, Ham concluded that the dog must have
returned.

He could kick himself for his begrudging
hospitality. If it were the dog whose visit the
night before had unsettled him, he really
should put him out of his misery. He did not
like the thought, but what could he do? With
some anger at being so put upon, he went
into the house, took the old shotgun from its
place in the corner, loaded it, picked up his
five cell flashlight again, and set out. Down
past the barn and through the pasture he
walked in the direction of the howling
sounds. The thin skiff of snow on the frozen
ground crunched under his feet.

A few yards beyond the barn in the pasture there was a small pond, covering not
more than two or three acres. The pasture
was bounded by a fence of five barbed wires
mounted on wooden posts. The fence cut
right through the pond on the lower side, a

29

30

few feet back from an earthen dam. It was situated so as to keep the cattle away from the dam and the rock lined spillway on one end where the water ran over in a big rain. Shining his flashlight along this fence, Ham saw the dog partially suspended on the top wires about midway across the frozen surface. He made his way around the upper end of the pond and down the opposite side to a spot close to the fence. His light showed clearly that it was indeed the very dog.

31

Standing beside the pond with the shotgun in his hand, an unlikely thought came to him. Perhaps he should try to save the animal. Ham tested the ice with his foot—a little weight, then some more. This was answered by a sharp cracking sound that sped outward and away, losing itself in the sound of the breeze. No, he could not risk walking on it. The freeze was too recent; the ice too new. The water was shallow of course, but to break through and get soaking wet would expose him to severe cold in the breeze, maybe even frost bite, before he could reach the house.

The middle of the dam was closer to the dog than this place where he stood, but he still would have to wade. The only way a rescue could be achieved was by walking out to the center of the pond somehow on the wire of the fence. The bottom strand of the five wires plus two shorter strands which had been attached below it in the dry season were all frozen under the ice. However, the one just above it was two or three inches above the ice. By stepping on this and holding on to the top wire with his back to the pond, he could step slowly sideways. That way only his heels and part of his weight would be on the ice. He didn't like this at all, but the howling of the dog continued, lower now and sounding more pitiable than before.

What happened next is mysterious. To say that it was uncharacteristic of Ham is to trivialize. Something unforeseen must have prompted him. He laid down the old shotgun and the flashlight in the snow, grasped the top wire in his gloved hands, and start inching his way toward the dog. He could feel the barbed wire tearing at the front of his coat.

As he drew closer, within a few feet of the dog, the top wire seemed to spring more toward him, making it quite difficult to proceed. He began to include the next wire down in his grasp. Then he could see clearly what had happened. The top wire was loose from some of the posts. The dog in chasing a rabbit or something had raced over the ice and attempted a climbing leap over the fence. The loose top wire had sprung downward below the next wire and then, creating a barbed vice-like effect, had trapped both front feet between the barbs of the two strands. His hind feet touched the ice, but this provided no traction.

The disentanglement was hard. It was difficult to hold on to the wire with one hand

33

and separate the springy wires with the other. The dog was completely limp now, hanging from his snare in total exhaustion. He emitted low moaning sounds; he was still alive. Ham persisted, and in another minute or two the dog fell onto the ice. Just then Ham noticed a stinging sensation on the inside of his hand. In spite of his great care in grasping the wire, one or two of the barbs had penetrated his glove and punctured his left hand. The pain was not severe but none the less annoying as he held to the fence and inched his way back across the ice to the edge of the pond, dragging the dog with him. There he picked up the dog. He was surprised by his weight. He must have weighed at least forty-five pounds. Ham placed the flashlight in one of his pockets. His old shotgun was left laying in the snow as he carried the dog slowly back around the far end of the pond and up the gradual slope toward the house.

Brief rest stops were made along the way.

34

He was by this time almost exhausted. As he walked, a curious dialogue went on inside his head. What had he done extending himself in this way? He was an utter fool. Yet, here he was laboring with his strange burden up through the pasture toward the house. And what would he do with the dog now? Should he take him further away? Twenty miles? A hundred? Should he go back for the gun and destroy him after saving him? There were no answers.

Then too, there was the matter of the blood. The dog was bleeding from both fore legs. He himself was wounded in his hand, wounded and bleeding from the sharp barbs of the fence. As he paused another time to rest, the strangest thought of all laid hold of him. He and this dog were bleeding together! There was a strange oneness to their pain. Though Ham was anything but a mystic, the realization of the commonality of their life— his and the dogs—invaded his thinking.

35

36

Once inside the back entry way, he removed his gloves and examined his hand. The puncture marks made by the wire were up and slightly to the left of the center of the palm. Taking a pan of warm water and pouring in some Lysol, he began to wash the legs and stomach of the dog. He was fearful that bacteria of some kind would enter the wound in his hand. The dog did not protest, remaining still on the entry way floor. When this task was finished he took more water in a different pan and washed his hands thoroughly and soaked the punctures with peroxide. He dried them carefully and bandaged the puncture marks. He then taped up the dogs legs and carried him through to the front entry way. Ham then remembered that there was some blood on his coat. Removing the insulated lining he put the coat to soak in a large bucket.

All of this done, Ham stirred the fire a bit, sat down in his chair and reflected. He thought and thought about things. He won-

37

dered most of all about himself. Who was he, and what was he becoming?

Now, there was something else also. A strong feeling took hold of him that he should go to the church and receive communion. But was this right? Was he worthy? Of course not! He was quite sure he was not worthy, but the inner urge grew stronger. And another question: Could he face the curious stares of his neighbors? He convinced himself that none of these things mattered. He looked at the clock. It was eleven thirty-five. Too late! Even so, he bent down and quickly unlaced his boots and removed them. His pants seemed clean enough; anyway there was not time to change. He grabbed different shoes and a better coat, a dry one, and in ten minutes was driving the three miles to the church.

The church windows glowed faintly, indicating candle light inside. The small parking lot was full of cars with a few also parked

38

along the road. Turning into the driveway with the intent of backing out and turning back to park beside the road, he was surprised to see that there was one position open in the lot itself, the fifth position from the far end facing the cemetery fence. It occurred to him that this spot must be close to Josie's grave. How strange he thought that this was the only vacant space in the lot! Someone must have parked there earlier and then left the service for some reason. He drove in toward it. Surely enough, he was directly in front of the grave which was just inside the fence. The truck lights illuminated the stone:

39

Josephine Carrel
1907-1945
Beloved Wife of Hamilton Carrel

He sat and looked at the stone, wondering. Then he turned off the lights, got out of the truck, moved forward, and stood holding to the top of the wrought iron fence. He felt pain in his left palm as he did so. In a few sec

40

onds, after his eyes accustomed themselves to the darkness, the stone seemed to gather a light from somewhere, a faint golden glow. He stood transfixed. How could this be? Turning and looking behind him, he saw that the lights had been turned on inside the church. The faint light on the stone had apparently come from a yellow section in one of the stained glass windows. Though he had promised himself long ago that he would not mourn the loss of Josie, his eyes welled up—his cheeks felt cold from the wetness of tears.

After this brief time by the fence, he turned and walked across the lot and entered the small vestibule of the church. He quietly opened the inner door and looked in. The little church was full. The people were standing, but it appeared that there were two vacant chairs along the back wall. As he went to one of them he caught the words of the unison voices: "...the communion of the saints; the forgiveness of sins; the resurrec

41

42

tion of the body and the life everlasting. Amen." Then the people were seated.

Ham looked around. He did not recognize those seated on either side of him. However, those in the two or three seats ahead of him and those on either side of the center aisle were known to him. They were all his neighbors.

Across the aisle and four benches up, a younger couple sat: the Jensens with their two children. They were beautiful children! The mother had her arm on the back of the bench behind the children and was stroking the father's shoulder. Ham was moved by the simplicity of this act. He felt a deep longing for Josie. Then just ahead of him and across the aisle he saw Mary Hessert, Frank Hessert's widow. He was struck by how pretty she was. This thought surprised him. It had not entered his mind before.

When the pastor had finished reading the words of preparation, the lights were turned

43

off again, and the warm glow of the candles lighted the room. The words of Silent Night were sung. The people in the front rows went and knelt at the rail. Others behind them did the same in their turn, and finally the turn came for those in the very back. Ham followed others forward. He was keenly aware that people were watching him, perhaps even with unkind thoughts. It did not matter to him now. Nothing mattered except this deep desire to reconnect with something or someone. Inside this little church, the dim light of the candles lighted the darkness of his spirit. Their warmth was slowly melting the coldness of his heart. He felt close to Josie now. True, her body was out there beneath the mound beyond the fence. Yet, she was here—in the room and in his heart.

44

Thus, on December 24 of the year 1975, Hamilton Carrel knelt at the rail of the church. The belated prodigal was home.

After the singing of a stanza of another

carol and a cheery benediction from the pastor, the lights were turned up, and the people moved out. Ham was first out because of his advantageous seat near the door. Besides, he preferred not to see anyone.

Yet as he walked toward the car, he heard a voice call, "Ham!"

He turned and saw the Jensens, Paul, his wife, and the two children. Paul held out his hand. Ham took it. Paul Jensen said only three words.

"Merry Christmas, Ham!"

Then one of the children, the little girl, stretched her hand upward toward Ham. He wrapped his large hand around her small, soft one.

"Merry Christmas!" she said.

This was too much for Ham. He was almost overcome. He turned and walked across to his truck. Backing it out carefully,

45

46

he drove away from the little church toward home.

Once there, he went through to the front without removing his coat. The dog had recovered a bit, and in fact had pushed open the door of the entry way and situated himself closer to the fireplace. He raised his head and looked at Ham. Was it? Yes it must have been—a look of gratitude.

It would be wrong to claim that Ham was totally changed into a new self from this Christmas forward. From time to time, his old self would rise again. Even so, he had passed through some kind of door. And though it took several more years before he could close it behind him, he could not and would not go back again. He could still be bitter on occasion, but he no longer enjoyed it.

Neighbors noticed a difference in him right away. He would now wave to them when he drove past their houses in his pickup truck with that ugly dog of his riding in

47

the cab beside him. They would wave back. Sometimes he would stop and talk with them when he saw them in town.

Was all this in his mind—or perhaps in theirs? Who is to say? It was as though the whole neighborhood had changed with him.

It is a painful mystery why life's brokenness so often invades the human spirit—and a mystery how community is broken in turn. Yet even these do not match the strange mystery of grace. Not many of us to be sure will be called back to life by a stray dog, but the interventions of Providence are varied and wondrous altogether.

48

49

B. L. Bryan is available for personal appearances and/or speaking engagements. For more information, email an inquiry to Bill at: bryanbande@aol.com.

To order additional copies of this or other books call our toll-free ordering line: 1-888-383-3110 or visit our online bookstore at: www.advbooks.com.

Longwood, Florida, USA

"we bring dreams to life"™
www.advbooks.com

Printed in the United States
23922LVS00004B/1-2

9 780975 433249